JP Morgan Trading Losses: Implications for the Volcker Rule and Other Regulation

Gary Shorter
Specialist in Financial Economics

Edward V. Murphy
Specialist in Financial Economics

Rena S. Miller
Analyst in Financial Economics

August 16, 2012

Congressional Research Service
7-5700
www.crs.gov
R42665

CRS Report for Congress
Prepared for Members and Committees of Congress

Summary

On May 10, 2012, JP Morgan disclosed that it had lost more than $2 billion by trading financial derivatives. Jamie Dimon, CEO and chairman of JP Morgan, reported that the bank's Chief Investment Office (CIO) executed the trades to hedge the firm's overall credit exposure as part of the bank's asset liability management program (ALM). The CIO operated within the depository subsidiary of JP Morgan, although its offices were in London. The funding for the trades came from what JP Morgan characterized as excess deposits, which are the difference between deposits held by the bank and its commercial loans.

The trading losses resulted from an attempt to unwind a previous hedge investment, although the precise details remain unconfirmed. The losses occurred in part because the CIO chose to place a new counter-hedge position, rather than simply unwind the original position. In 2007 and 2008, JP Morgan had bought an index tied to credit default swaps on a broad index of high-grade corporate bonds. In general, this index would tend to protect JP Morgan if general economic conditions worsened (or systemic risk increased) because the perceived health of high-grade firms would tend to deteriorate with the economy. In 2011, the CIO decided to change the firm's position by implementing a new counter trade. Because this new trade was not identical to the earlier trades, it introduced basis risk and market risk, among other potential problems. It is this second "hedge on a hedge" that is responsible for the losses in 2012.

Several financial regulators are responsible for overseeing elements of the JP Morgan trading losses. The Office of the Comptroller of the Currency (OCC) is the primary prudential regulator of federally chartered depository banks and their ALM activities, including the CIO of JP Morgan, even though it is located in London. The Federal Reserve is the prudential regulator of JP Morgan's holding company, although it would tend to defer to the primary prudential regulators of the firm's subsidiaries for significant regulation of those entities. The Federal Reserve also regulates systemic risk aspects of large financial firms such as JP Morgan. The CIO must comply with Federal Deposit Insurance Corporation (FDIC) regulations because it is part of the insured depository. The Securities and Exchange Commission (SEC) oversees JP Morgan's required disclosures to the firm's stockholders regarding material risks and losses such as the trades. The Commodity Futures Trading Commission (CFTC) regulates trading in swaps and financial derivatives. The heads of these agencies coordinate through the Financial Stability Oversight Council (FSOC), which is chaired by the Secretary of Treasury.

The trading losses may have implications for a number of financial regulatory issues. For example, should the exemption to the Volcker Rule for hedging be interpreted broadly enough to encompass general portfolio hedges like the JP Morgan trades, or should hedging be limited to more specific risks? Are current regulations of large financial firms the appropriate balance to address perceptions that some firms are too-big-to-fail?

The trading losses raise concerns about the calculation and reporting of risk by large financial firms. JP Morgan changed its value at risk (VaR) model during the time of the trading losses. Some are concerned that VaR models may not adequately address potential risks. Some are concerned that the change in reporting of the VaR at JP Morgan's CIO may not have provided adequate disclosures of the potential risks that JP Morgan faced. Such disclosures are governed by securities laws.

Contents

Introduction 1
    Congressional Interest in JP Morgan's Trading Losses 4
    The Scope of this Report 4
JP Morgan and Its Chief Investment Office 5
The Alleged Growth in the CIO's Appetite for Risk 6
The Losing Trades 7
The Regulation of JP Morgan in the Context of the CIO's Trades 10
    Office of the Comptroller of the Currency 10
    Federal Reserve 11
    Federal Deposit Insurance Corporation 12
    General Concerns over the Bank Regulators and the JP Morgan Trades 12
    Securities and Exchange Commission 13
    Commodity Futures Trading Commission 14
"Too Big to Fail" and the Financial Stability Oversight Council 15
Systemic Implications of JP Morgan's Losses 17
The Potential Implications of JP Morgan's Losses for Other Large Banks 18
The Volcker Rule and JP Morgan's CIO Transactions 19
    Limits on Speculative Trades and Relationships by Banks 19
    JP Morgan Trading Losses in the Context of the Volcker Rule 23
Potential Risk Management Shortcomings Related to the CIO 24
    CEO Dimon Allegedly Pushes for a Greater Emphasis on Profits and Risk Taking in
        the CIO 25
    Potentially Lax and Ineffective Oversight 25
    Value at Risk Models and the CIO 28
    JP Morgan's Risk Management Committee 30

Figures

Figure 1. Regulators Related to JP Morgan Trades 10

Contacts

Author Contact Information 31

Introduction

JP Morgan Chase (JP Morgan), the nation's largest bank holding company by asset size,[1] had established a reputation for quality risk management.[2] On May 10, 2012, Jamie Dimon, the bank's chairman and chief executive officer (CEO),[3] held an unplanned conference call. As reflected in the firm's first quarter 2012 filings with the Securities and Exchange Commission (SEC), Mr. Dimon reported that, during the early part of the second quarter, a London-based office of the bank (insured depository) unit, the Chief Investment Office (CIO), sought "to hedge[4] the firm's overall credit exposure" and incurred "slightly more than [a] $2 billion trading [paper] loss on ... synthetic credit positions." The CEO characterized the trading strategy behind the loss as "flawed, complex, poorly reviewed, poorly executed and poorly monitored [and noted that] the portfolio has proven to be riskier, more volatile and less effective as economic hedge than we thought." He also said that the portfolio still contained securities with "a lot of risk and volatility going forward.... It could cost us as much as $1 billion or more.... [I]t is risky, and it will be for a couple of quarters."[5]

The loss was charged to the bank's corporate and private equity division, which houses the CIO. During the conference call, Mr. Dimon also indicated that the loss would be partially offset by a $1 billion gain from the sale of securities by the unit, resulting in an $800 million second quarter loss for the division.[6]

The May conference call occurred several weeks after a routine April 13, 2012, conference call in which Mr. Dimon reported on the bank's first-quarter earnings. During the April call, he referred to concerns raised over the bank's exposure to the money-losing trades (which he derided in the May call) as "a complete tempest in a teapot."[7]

---

[1] For example, see Alistair Osborne, "How Dimon was Knocked off his Pedestal by the London Whale," *The Daily Telegraph* (United Kingdom), May 12, 2012.

[2] For example, see David Henry, "JPMorgan Execs Set to Leave, Sources Say," *Reuters*, May 13, 2012, at http://www.reuters.com/article/2012/05/14/jpmorgan-departures-idUSL1E8GD3CW20120514.

[3] For years, activist shareholders have sought to get various companies to split the jobs of board chairman and corporate CEO. Their principal argument has been that the common practice of allowing one person to assume both roles undermines the independence and thus the effectiveness of corporate boards. §972 of the Dodd-Frank Wall Street Reform and Consumer Protection Act, H.Rept. 111-203, requires companies to disclose in their annual proxy report the reasons why the issuer has chosen the same person to serve as chairman of the board of directors and CEO or why the company has chosen to have different individuals fill those two positions. At the JP Morgan's annual shareholder meeting in May 2012, 40% of shareholder votes were reportedly in support of a proposal to split Mr. Dimon's role as chairman and CEO. Many of the votes were probably cast before news of the large trading losses. "JP Morgan faces FBI Investigation over Losses; Double Blow as 40pc of Shareholders Vote Against Jamie Dimon's Joint Role," *Daily Telegraph* (United Kingdom), May 16, 2012, p. 5.

[4] In simple terms, hedging is an attempt to offset or mitigate the risks from other sources or actions.

[5] Raw Transcript for JPMorgan Chase & Co., May 10, 2012, at http://i.mktw.net/_newsimages/pdf/jpm-conference-call.pdf.

[6] Ibid.

[7] For example, see "Meet the Press" transcript for May 13, 2012, in which Mr. Dimon acknowledged making the statement, at http://www.msnbc.msn.com/id/47403362/ns/meet_the_press-transcripts/t/may-reince-priebus-martin-omalley-gavin-newsom-al-cardenas-kathleen-parker-jonathan-capehart-chris-matthews-jamie-dimon/#.T7AdPlJ5EjEe. Also see Monica Langley, "Inside JP Morgan's Blunder," *Wall Street Journal*, May 18, 2012; and Peter Henning, "JPMorgan's Loss: Illegal, or Just Bad Judgment?," *The New York Times*, May 14, 2012, at http://dealbook.nytimes.com/2012/05/14/jpmorgans-loss-illegal-or-just-bad-judgment/?smid=tw-nytimesbusiness&seid=auto.

The losses described in the May conference call were mark-to-market paper losses[8] that had not been booked by the bank. While some analysts speculated that JP Morgan would not lose much more than the $2 billion,[9] others speculated that the bank would ultimately lose as much as $5 billion or more.[10] Final losses will depend on various unknowns, such as the proportion of the suspect trades that have not been liquidated or unwound, future movements of the indexes, the speed at which the bank tries to unwind those trades, and the size of the subsequent losses from the remaining positions. During the May conference call, Mr. Dimon said that the bank would be unwinding the trades in a deliberate manner.[11]

During a subsequent conference call on July 13, 2012, bank officials detailed key developments during the second quarter of 2012. During the call, Mr. Dimon indicated, with respect to the suspect trades, the CIO lost $1.6 billion and $4.4 billion, respectively, during the first and second quarters of 2012. Mr. Dimon also indicated that the CIO's total trading risk in the trades had been "significantly reduced."[12]

JP Morgan's shareholders have borne and will bear the impact of losses. The day after the May conference call, JP Morgan's stock price fell by about 9% and the value of its market capitalization fell by about $14 billion.[13] On May 21, 2012, the bank announced that it was suspending a previously planned $15 billion stock buyback that regulators from the Federal Reserve approved in March 2012 after performing stress tests on the bank's capital. At about the same time, the bank decided to maintain its quarterly dividend of $0.30 a share.[14] Buybacks can help boost the price of a company's shares. Since the May conference call, several class action shareholders suits, alleging that the bank misled investors, have also been filed.[15]

According to news reports, after the conference call, Fitch Ratings, a major credit rating agency, downgraded JP Morgan's short-term and long-term debt by a notch. Both are still categorized as investment grade debt. The reports also indicated that Fitch indicated that the $2 billion loss was "manageable." The rating agency also noted that the size of the loss and the "ongoing nature of

---

[8] A paper loss is an unrealized loss that has not yet been officially booked as an accounting loss.

[9] "Wall Street Puzzles over Size of JP Morgan's Potential Trading Loss," *Reuters*, May 20, 2012, at http://www.iol.co.za/business/features/wall-street-puzzles-over-size-of-jpmorgan-s-potential-trading-loss-1.1300253.

[10] Erik Kobayashi-Solomon, "The Moral of J.P. Morgan's Derivative Debacle," *Morningstar*, May 23, 2012, a at http://news.morningstar.com/articlenet/article.aspx?id=554917.

[11] Raw Transcript for JPMorgan Chase & Co., May 10, 2012.

[12] Transcript of JP Morgan's Conference Call, July 13, 2012, at http://w3.nexis.com/new/results/docview/docview.do?docLinkInd=true&risb=21_T15146317360&format=GNBFI&sort=BOOLEAN&startDocNo=1&resultsUrlKey=29_T15146317341&cisb=22_T15146317340&treeMax=true&treeWidth=0&csi=254610&docNo=3.

[13] Prial Dunstan, "JP Morgan Gaffe is an Argument for Capital, Not the Volcker Rule," May 21, 2012, at http://www.foxbusiness.com/industries/2012/05/11/jpmorgan-losses-argument-for-capital-not-volcker-rule/. In addition, on May 21, 2012, Mr. Dimon announced that JP Morgan was suspending a previously planned $15 billion stock buyback plan because "we want to box this thing [with respect to the trading losses] first." Robin Sidel and Dan Fitzpatrick, "J.P. Morgan Suspends Share Buyback," *Wall Street Journal*, May 21, 2012, at http://online.wsj.com/article/SB10001424052702303610504577418100138866184.html?mod=WSJ_hp_LEFTWhatsNewsCollection.

[14] "JPMorgan Chase & Co. Stops Stock Buybacks," *Reuters*, May 21, 2012, at http://www.reuters.com/finance/stocks/JPM/key-developments/article/2544789.

[15] For example, see "Robbins Geller Rudman & Dowd LLP Files," May 14, 2012, at http://www.rgrdlaw.com/cases-jpmorganchase.html. Also see "Bernstein Liebhard LLP Announces that a Securities Class Action Has Been Filed Against JP Morgan Chase & Co.," May 15, 2012, at http://www.bloomberg.com/article/2012-05-15/a.BarQ1g2hrs.html.

these positions implies a lack of liquidity [and that the loss] also raised questions over JPM's risk appetite, risk management framework, and its practices and oversight."[16]

Several bank analysts have indicated that the report of the losses raised concerns about the quality of JP Morgan's risk management. However, there appears to be general consensus that the losses are relatively small when compared with the size of the bank's overall balance sheet.[17] This view appears to be shared by officials at the Office of the Comptroller of the Currency (OCC), the financial regulator that oversees JP Morgan's national bank and various subsidiaries. On June 6, 2012, Comptroller of the Currency Thomas Curry testified that, "given the scale of the bank, the loss by JPMC affects its earnings, but does not present a solvency issue."[18]

The May conference call had a variety of other ripple effects both inside and outside of JP Morgan. The head of the bank's CIO stepped down. JP Morgan is conducting internal investigations of the losses, which are being overseen by the company's board. One outcome of the probe, *The CIO Task Force Update*, was completed in July 2012. Among other things, the report, which described itself as a product of a JP Morgan "management review and assessment of circumstances surrounding the CIO's losses," criticized the CIO for "ineffective" risk management and exercising "poor" judgment with respect to various trades during the first quarter of 2012.[19]

Mr. Dimon also indicated that the board of directors would be examining whether bank employees responsible for the losses would be subject to the bank's heretofore unused compensation "clawback" policy. The policy enables the bank to require the return of certain compensation given to senior employees, including "unvested stock" and "cash bonuses," following actions deemed to be unsatisfactory, including "bad judgment."[20]

---

[16] According to other news reports, while affirming the bank's investment grade A rating, Standard & Poor's, another major credit rating agency cited JP Morgan's potential for broader problems from its hedging strategies. It indicated that the strategies were not "consistent with what we have viewed as the company's sound risk-management practices." Michael Moore, "Fitch Cuts JPMorgan Rating as S&P Calls Outlook Negative," *Bloomberg*, May 12, 2012, at http://www.bloomberg.com/news/2012-05-11/jpmorgan-credit-rating-reduced-by-fitch-on-2-billion-loss-1-.html.

[17] For example, see "Analyst Downgrades Of JP Morgan Stock Stay Scarce," *Dow Jones Newswire*, May 23, 2012, at http://www.nasdaq.com/article/analyst-downgrades-of-jp-morgan-stock-stay-scarce-20120511-01135.

[18] Testimony of Thomas J. Curry, Comptroller of the Currency, before the Senate Committee on Banking, Housing, and Urban Affairs, June 6, 2012, available at http://www.occ.gov/news-issuances/congressional-testimony/2012/pub-test-2012-86-written.pdf - 2012-06-06.

[19] "CIO Task Force Update," July 13, 2012, at http://investor.shareholder.com/jpmorganchase/secfiling.cfm?FilingID=19617-12-248.

[20] "Senate Committee on Banking, Housing, and Urban Affairs Holds a Hearing on JP Morgan's Trading Loss," *Political Transcript Wire*, June 13, 2012, at http://search.proquest.com/docview/1020124449/138004078AC4665D817/50?accountid=12084. Under §304 of the Sarbanes-Oxley Act of 2002 (SOX, P.L. 107-204), a public company is entitled to require its CEO and its chief finance officer to repay to the company previously received incentive-based compensation when the company has had to issue a financial restatement "as the result of misconduct." The Dodd-Frank Act of 2012 expanded on that. §953 directed stock exchanges to adopt listing standards that require current or former executive officers to repay erroneously awarded incentive compensation when their company restates their accounting disclosure due to "material noncompliance" with federal securities laws. The executives are required to return incentive-based compensation received during the three-year period before the restatement that is in excess of what they would have received had the original financial statement been accurate.

Meanwhile, OCC officials have indicated that the agency is "evaluating the compensation process of the CIO and will assess the bank's determination on clawbacks as part of that analysis [and] if corrective action is warranted."[21]

Various agencies, including the United Kingdom's financial services regulator (the Financial Services Administration), the SEC, the Commodities Futures Trading Commission (CFTC), the Federal Reserve (the Fed), the OCC, and the Federal Deposit Insurance Corporation (FDIC), have launched probes of various aspects of the trades. The Department of Justice (DOJ)[22] and the Federal Bureau of Investigation (FBI) have begun probes aimed at determining whether there was criminal wrongdoing surrounding the trades.[23]

Congressional Interest in JP Morgan's Trading Losses

Congress has held hearings that have both touched on and been exclusively devoted to JP Morgan's trading losses. Key congressional interest derives from two broad concerns: (1) what the losses may help reveal about the efficacy of bank regulatory monitoring and oversight; and (2) potential insights that the losses may provide on implementation of various provisions in the Dodd-Frank Wall Street Reform and Consumer Protection Act (DFA; P.L. 111-203).

The Scope of this Report

This report provides general background on JP Morgan and its regulation; the CIO, the unit responsible for the losing trades; and the losing trades themselves. It examines various aspects of JP Morgan's operations with respect to the trades.

This report is drawn from media reports, congressional testimony, and other sources. It will be updated as information from governmental investigations, shareholder lawsuits, official reports from JP Morgan, and other investigations develops.

The report also examines several public policy issues involving large banks such as JP Morgan that have become more visible due to the trading losses. These issues include

- potential regulatory lapses and shortcomings in the regulatory reach;
- risk management at JP Morgan's CIO;
- Section 619 of the DFA, also known as the Volcker Rule;
- systemic significance of the losses;
- potential broader implications of the losses for other large banks; and
- the doctrine of "too big to fail" in the context of the JP Morgan trade losses.

---

[21] Testimony of Thomas J. Curry, Comptroller of the Currency, before the Senate Committee on Banking, Housing, and Urban Affairs, June 6, 2012, available at http://www.occ.gov/news-issuances/congressional-testimony/2012/pub-test-2012-86-written.pdf - 2012-06-06.

[22] For example, see Katy Burne, Aaron Lucchetti, and Gregory Zuckerman, "Hedge or Bet? Parsing a Trade. J.P. Morgan Moves Raise Questions About Its Strategy," *Wall Street Journal*, May 16, 2012.

[23] For example, see "FBI's Mueller Confirms JPMorgan Preliminary Probe," *Reuters*, May 16, 2012, at http://www.newsdaily.com/stories/bre84f0ti-us-jpmorgan-fbi/.

JP Morgan and Its Chief Investment Office

JP Morgan conducts business in some 60 countries, has more than $2 trillion in assets, and maintains 5,500 bank branches. The JP Morgan of today began as JP Morgan, a commercial bank, in the 19th century. It has subsequently grown into a diversified financial complex through a series of acquisitions and mergers that have included Chase Manhattan, a commercial bank; Bear Stearns, an investment bank; and the banking operations of Washington Mutual, a thrift institution.[24] In 2011, JP Morgan reported gross profits of about $99 billion and net profits of $19 billion. The bank engages in mortgage lending, credit card issuance, investment banking, and asset management.[25] It is also serves as a primary dealer in U.S. government securities. Overall, the financial services company has several broad business lines: (1) retail financial services, (2) treasury and securities services, (3) card services, (4) investment banking, (5) commercial banking, (6) asset management, and (7) corporate/private equity.

The Chief Investment Office (CIO) is a part of the corporate/private equity line, which also houses the company's risk management unit, the private-equity arm, and the treasury office. The CIO is tasked with the responsibility of "managing structural interest rate, currency and certain credit risks that are created from the day-to-day operations of the firm's primary lines of business across the company."[26] The unit also "manages the [JP Morgan] firm's investment exposure while helping to advise lines of business on their own investment strategies [and] is responsible for managing the firm's interest rate risk, foreign exchange risk and other structural risks, each of which are critical measures for the firm."[27]

In congressional testimony on June 13, 2012, Mr. Dimon spoke about the CIO's mission and the scope of its activities:

> Like many banks, we have more deposits than loans—at quarter end, we held approximately $1.1 trillion in deposits and $700 billion in loans. CIO, along with our Treasury unit, invests excess cash in a portfolio that includes Treasuries, agencies, mortgage-backed securities, high quality securities, corporate debt and other domestic and overseas assets. This portfolio serves as an important source of liquidity and maintains an average rating of AA+. It also serves as an important vehicle for managing the assets and liabilities of the consolidated company. In short, the bulk of CIO's responsibility is to manage an approximately $350 billion portfolio.[28]

---

[24] See History of the JP Morgan Firm, available at http://www.jpmorganchase.com/corporate/About-JPMC/jpmorgan-history.htm.

[25] "JP Morgan & Chase Company Profile," *Hoovers*, at http://www.hoovers.com/company/Jpmorgan_Chase__Co/rfytti-1.html.

[26] See the 2012 Schedule 14A Proxy Statement Pursuant to §14(a) of the Securities Exchange Act of 1934 for JP Morgan Chase, at http://www.sec.gov/Archives/edgar/data/19617/000001961712000185/jpmc2012proxystatement.htm.

[27] JP Morgan Chase Notice of 2012 Annual Meeting of Shareholders and Proxy Statement, April 4, 2012, at http://files.shareholder.com/downloads/ONE/1895794676x0x556146/e8b56256-365c-45aa-bbdb-3aa82f0d07ea/JPMC_2012_proxy_statement.pdf.

[28] Testimony of Jamie Dimon, chairman and CEO, JP Morgan Chase & Co., before the Senate Committee on Banking, Housing and Urban Affairs, June 13, 2012, at http://blogs.wsj.com/deals/2012/06/12/jamie-dimons-testimony-traders-didnt-understand-the-risk/?mod=google_news_blog.

Before Jamie Dimon became the bank's CEO, JP Morgan's CIO was not a discrete unit, but was part of the bank's treasury unit. As is the case with bank chief investment offices, bank treasury units are also concerned with asset/liability management.[29]

Other large banking complexes have functions that are similar to what JP Morgan's CIO does, but many have organized them differently. For example, media accounts indicate that Bank of America has a chief investment officer who reports to the company's chief financial officer (CFO). Citigroup's treasurer is reported to directly oversee a comparable portfolio through his oversight of the bank's chief investment office as well as deputy treasurers in other countries. In addition, according to some reports, at Wells Fargo, the CIO is divided between the CFO and the head of the investment banking and trading division.[30] Citigroup apparently has a centralized office that reports to its treasurer to hedge liability risks for the New York bank, but lacks an individual unit that engages in the kind of macroeconomic hedging that JP Morgan's CIO officially does.[31]

According to various reports, but unconfirmed by the Congressional Research Service (CRS), a major difference between JP Morgan's CIO and comparable units at other large banks involves the composition of their portfolios. Similar units at other large banks are said to hold smaller proportions of relatively risky instruments than JP Morgan's CIO and tend to have "financial filings [that indicate] that their holdings are concentrated in low-risk, low-return assets such as Treasuries, government-backed mortgages and corporate and municipal bonds."[32]

The Alleged Growth in the CIO's Appetite for Risk

After becoming JP Morgan's CEO in 2005, Jamie Dimon hired Ina Drew, a veteran trader and manager, to head the CIO.[33] According to media accounts, Ms. Drew reported directly to Mr. Dimon.[34] Former JP Morgan employees who worked with Ms. Drew have told reporters that she received the CEO's authorization to ramp up the unit's investments in relatively risky financial products such as asset-backed securities, equities, credit derivatives, and nations' sovereign debt.[35]

---

[29] For example, see Vincent Ryan, "JP Morgan Hedge Exposed the Bank to More Risk," *CFO.com*, May 16, 2012, at http://www3.cfo.com/Print/PrintArticle?pageId=36516aaf-3512-4176-89e8-8ac5521fe277.

[30] For example, see Bradley Keoun, Donal Griffin and Michael J. Moore, "JP Morgan Veered From Hedging Practices at Competing Banks," *Bloomberg*, May 22, 2012, at http://mobile.bloomberg.com/news/2012-05-22/jpmorgan-veered-from-hedging-practices-at-competing-banks?category=%2Fnews%2Fmostread%2F.

[31] Robin Sidel, Aaron Lucchetti, and Liz Rappaport, "Reputation Is Staff Concern; Wall Street Rivals Fret About Tougher Regulation, Possible Credit Downgrades," *Wall Street Journal*, May 13, 2012, at http://www.businessdictionary.com/definition/risk-management.html#ixzz1vuzCizlO.

[32] For example, see Christian Berthelsen, "JP Morgan Chase Faces Risk In Managing Derivative Trades," *Dow Jones*, May 11, 2012, Available at http://online.wsj.com/article/BT-CO-20120511-715864.html.

[33] Dawn Kopecki and Max Abelson, "Dimon Fortress Breached as Push From Hedges to Bets Blows Up," *Bloomberg*, May 14, 2012. at http://www.bloomberg.com/news/2012-05-14/dimon-fortress-breached-as-push-from-hedging-to-betting-blows-up.html.

[34] For example, see Eleanor Bloxham, "J.P. Morgan's Debacle: It's Time to Talk Exec Pay," *CNN/Money*, June 14, 2012, at http://management.fortune.cnn.com/2012/06/14/j-p-morgans-debacle-its-time-to-talk-exec-pay/.

[35] Ibid.

Financial reporting for the bank's corporate/private equity line of business is divided between the private equity side and the corporate side. JP Morgan's CIO and its treasury unit are the only money-making units in the corporate unit. According to the bank's financial disclosures from 2008 to 2011, the corporate unit reported net income of, respectively, $1.2 billion, $3.1 billion, $670 million, and $411 million.[36] During those years, the CIO was widely characterized as a significant "profit center" for the bank.[37] According to JP Morgan's financial filings, Ms. Drew earned $15 million in 2010 and $14 million in 2011, making her one of the company's highest paid officials.[38]

In 2006, Ms. Drew hired Achilles Macris to supervise trading in the CIO in London. Various reports have alleged that, with Mr. Dimon's approval, the London unit expanded into riskier types of derivatives. In 2011, in what some suggest may have reflected aggressive risk taking, Macris is claimed to have halted the use of risk-control caps, which had required traders to exit positions when their losses exceeded $20 million.[39] In June 2012 testimony, Mr. Dimon denied the assertion that the caps were removed.[40] In July 2012, however, a report on the bank's internal probe of the trades, *the CIO Task Force Update*, stated that the securities that had caused the CIO's trading losses were subject to "no limits by size, asset type or risk factor" for trading in the securities that resulted in the losses.

According to media reports, in late March 2012, the London unit began experiencing big trading day gains that were often followed by larger losses on the following day. As reported in an article in the *New York Times* during the period, Mr. Dimon was assured by Ms. Drew and her associates that the volatility was "manageable." According to the reports, extreme trading patterns, but with fewer gains offsetting the losses, reappeared a few days after JP Morgan reported its first quarter financials on April 13, 2012. Mr. Dimon's subsequent investigation of the situation reportedly revealed a problematic trading scenario in the CIO's London office. The May 2012 conference call in which Mr. Dimon reported the multi-billion dollar trading loss then followed.[41]

The Losing Trades

Several media articles have attempted to chronicle the nature of the CIO's trades that culminated in the bank's large losses. Using a combination of techniques, including discussions with the CIO's trading counterparties and analysis of the markets surrounding the alleged trades, the

---

[36] See also JP Morgan Chase Annual Report for 2010, at http://files.shareholder.com/downloads/ONE/1898236356x0x458380/ab2612d5-3629-46c6-ad94-5fd3ac68d23b/2010_JPMC_AnnualReport_.pdf; and JP Morgan Chase Annual Report for 2011, at http://files.shareholder.com/downloads/ONE/1898204862x0x556139/75b4bd59-02e7-4495-a84c-06e0b19d6990/JPMC_2011_annual_report_complete.pdf.

[37] For example, see Gregory Zuckerman, "From 'Caveman' to Whale' J.P. Morgan's Iksil Wagered Large, and Won, Last Year, but Bets in 2012 Soured," *Wall Street Journal*, May 17, 2012, at http://online.wsj.com/article/SB10001424052702303879604577408621039204432.html.

[38] See JP Morgan Chase Annual Report for 2010 and JP Morgan Chase Annual Report for 2011.

[39] For example, see Monica Langley, "Inside J.P. Morgan's Blunder," *Wall Street Journal*, May 18, 2012, at http://online.wsj.com/article/SB10001424052702303448404577410341236847980.html.

[40] "Senate Committee on Banking, Housing, and Urban Affairs Holds a Hearing on JP Morgan's Trading Loss," *Political Transcript Wire*, June 13, 2012.

[41] Jessica Silver-Greenberg and Nelson D. Schwartz, "Red Flags Said to Go Unheeded by Bosses at JPMorgan," *The New York Times*, May 14, 2012, at http://dealbook.nytimes.com/2012/05/14/warnings-said-to-go-unheeded-by-chase-bosses/.

authors of the articles have pieced together a common narrative on the likely nature of the losing trades.

However, as one such article noted, the "details [of the trades] remain obscure."[42] To date, the most authoritative, albeit general, discussion of the losing trades comes from two sources. These are congressional testimony from JP Morgan's Michael Cavanagh, CEO of the company's Treasury and Securities Services, and from Thomas Curry, Comptroller of the Currency, the head of the OCC, which regulates national banks and had examiners at JP Morgan when the trades occurred.

Discussing findings in JP Morgan's *CIO Task Force Update* during a July 12, 2012, conference call, JP Morgan's Cavanagh observed,

> The [synthetic credit portfolio's] primary purpose had been to provide a partial offset to losses we would suffer elsewhere in CIO, and the Company, in a stressed credit environment. The portfolio got started about five years ago. It was generally short credit. But also included some long positions in order to reduce the cost of carrying credit protection. And consistent with its objective, the portfolio produced gains in the stressed period of 2008 to 2010, and was breakeven or positive from each year from 2007 to 2011, and all-in, it generated about $2 billion in gains during that period....
>
> In late 2011, CIO was directed to reduce the synthetic credit portfolio's risk and risk weighted assets. That direction came as part of the annual budgeting process, in which we develop the firm's capital plans including our glide path to Basel III. [T]he synthetic credit team and CIO hoped to ... move their portfolio's risk position from a net short position to a neutral one, while reducing risk weighted assets in the process. They also hoped to retain some protection against Corporate credit defaults which was a synthetic credit portfolio's historical mission. So a lot of things going on that they were trying to accomplish, and found it difficult to find a balance that they liked.
>
> To simplify what they did, it amounted to them going long investment grade indices while increasing short positions in junior tranches in high yield indices. And the size of the portfolio grew dramatically as they continued to add positions later in the quarter, when they were struggling to balance the portfolio, as the market began to move against them. So a question of why they didn't just pursue an outright reduction of the portfolio. And it appears, and that's all it is, an appearance, that they thought about it a bit but they believed that it would be more expensive than the approach they chose, which obviously proved to be wrong, and were focused on thinking about high execution costs to reduce the portfolio in

---

[42] Matthew Weinschenk, "How JPMorgan's 'London Whale' Lost $2 Billion," *Wall Street Daily*, May 15th, 2012, at http://www.wallstreetdaily.com/2012/05/15/how-jpmorgans-london-whale-lost-2-billion. A fairly typical example of a common journalistic narrative on how JP Morgan's trades may have gone bad is as follows: "The chief investment office was making both bullish and bearish bets on corporate debt, using an index of credit derivatives [CDS] called the CDX IG Series 9 [an index that tracked the investment grade bonds of 121 companies, including Hewlett Packard, McDonald's, Macy's, and American Express]. It appears the bullish bet started to prompt big losses toward the end of April. At the time, the CDX index showed that the cost of insuring against company defaults was rising, a bearish signal. Given the size of the losses, people involved in the market surmise that JPMorgan's bullish bet is substantially bigger than its bearish bet. It is unclear just how large JPMorgan's position is, but people involved in the market figure the bank dominates this part of the credit market. So even small moves in the index can prove costly to JPMorgan. In addition, some analysts said they think JPMorgan focused its bearish bets on CDX indexes that mature within the next 12 months, while its bullish bets were on indexes that do not mature for a number of years. That mismatch could leave JPMorgan more exposed if the corporate market deteriorates." Peter Eavis, "How Bank Handles Its Bad Bet Is Fraught With Potential Peril," *The New York Times*, May 15, 2012.

size and the loss carry of a reduced portfolio, and so they went ahead with the approach they had....

[W]hat they did do was [to] increase the size and complexity of the portfolio dramatically in the first quarter [of 2012], and along with it, the sensitivity to a variety of risks ... all of which contributed in some part to the losses.... [With respect to] the growth of the portfolio in the first quarter ... the total notional size of the portfolio ... tripled. [The] significantly increased size and complexity of the portfolio left little margin for error when the expected pricing relationships across the portfolio began to break down and generate losses. It was a very risky approach they took that should have been discussed and vetted at more senior levels but it was not ....

... [The] portfolio experienced losses in late March and early April. Around this time, market visibility of the synthetic credit positions becomes a concern, particularly after press reports on April 6. At that point, Doug and Jamie asked for a review of the portfolio in preparation for the earnings release a few days later. Ina spear-headed the review with engagement by John Hogan, Doug Braunstein, and others. The main output of that review was forward scenario analysis that produced a probable P&L range for the second quarter on the portfolio from positive $350 million to negative $250 million, with a bias to the positive end. So at that time, the group got comfortable that the portfolio's risk was manageable, though in need of heightened attention going forward....

... On April 13, this period ends and we announce our first-quarter results.... In late April, losses pick up and the heightened monitoring that followed the earnings call gets taken to another level, when a senior team from Corporate Risk is sent to examine the portfolio from the bottom up. They begin providing daily updates and constructing independent analysis of the portfolio that becomes the basis for risk measurements that the new CIO team picks up a few weeks later....[43]

According to Comptroller of the Currency Curry,

In 2007 and 2008, the bank constructed a portfolio designed to partially offset credit risk using credit default swaps[44] to help protect the company from potential credit losses in a stressed global economy.... In late 2011 and early 2012, bank management revised its strategy and decided to offset its original position and reduce the amount of stress loss protection. The instruments chosen by the bank to execute the strategy were not identical to the instruments used in the original position, which introduced basis, liquidity, and other risks. As the new strategy was executed in the first quarter, actual performance deviated from expectations, and resulted in substantial losses in the second quarter....[45]

---

[43] See the comments of Mr. Cavanagh in: Transcript of JP Morgan Chase's Conference Call, July 13, 2012, at http://w3.nexis.com/new/results/docview/docview.do?docLinkInd=true&risb=21_T15146317360&format=GNBFI& sort=BOOLEAN&startDocNo=1&resultsUrlKey=29_T15146317341&cisb=22_T15146317340&treeMax=true& treeWidth=0&csi=254610&docNo=3.

[44] In a credit default swap "one party promises to pay another party if a third party defaults. The third party, in this case, is known as the 'reference entity.' The more technical definition of a credit default swap is a bilateral derivative contract that transfers from one party to another the risk that a specified reference entity will experience a 'credit event.' (Credit events may include default, bankruptcy, restructuring, or credit rating downgrade). Typically, the protection buyer pays a periodic fee to a protection seller in return for compensation if the reference entity experiences a credit event. The reference entity, such as a large firm that has issued a bond or a trust that has issued a mortgage-backed security ... is not a party to the credit default swap contract." CRS Report RS22932, *Credit Default Swaps: Frequently Asked Questions*, by Edward V. Murphy and Rena S. Miller.

[45] Testimony of Thomas J. Curry, Comptroller of the Currency before the Senate Committee on Banking, Housing, and Urban Affairs, *CQ Congressional Testimony*, June 6, 2012.

The Regulation of JP Morgan in the Context of the CIO's Trades

JP Morgan is generally regarded as a complex financial institution; the regulation of JP Morgan is similarly multifaceted. JP Morgan's organizational structure starts with a financial holding company, which controls a variety of subsidiaries, each with its own focus within the financial services industry. JP Morgan's holding company and many of its subsidiaries have their own primary prudential regulators, depending upon the financial service that they provide. In addition, many financial activities are subject to regulation regardless of the entity that carries it out. **Figure 1** illustrates how different financial regulatory agencies are responsible for prudential regulation of the units of JP Morgan that are believed to have carried out the derivatives trades, and the way that financial regulatory agencies regulate derivatives trading activities and venues.

Figure 1. Regulators Related to JP Morgan Trades

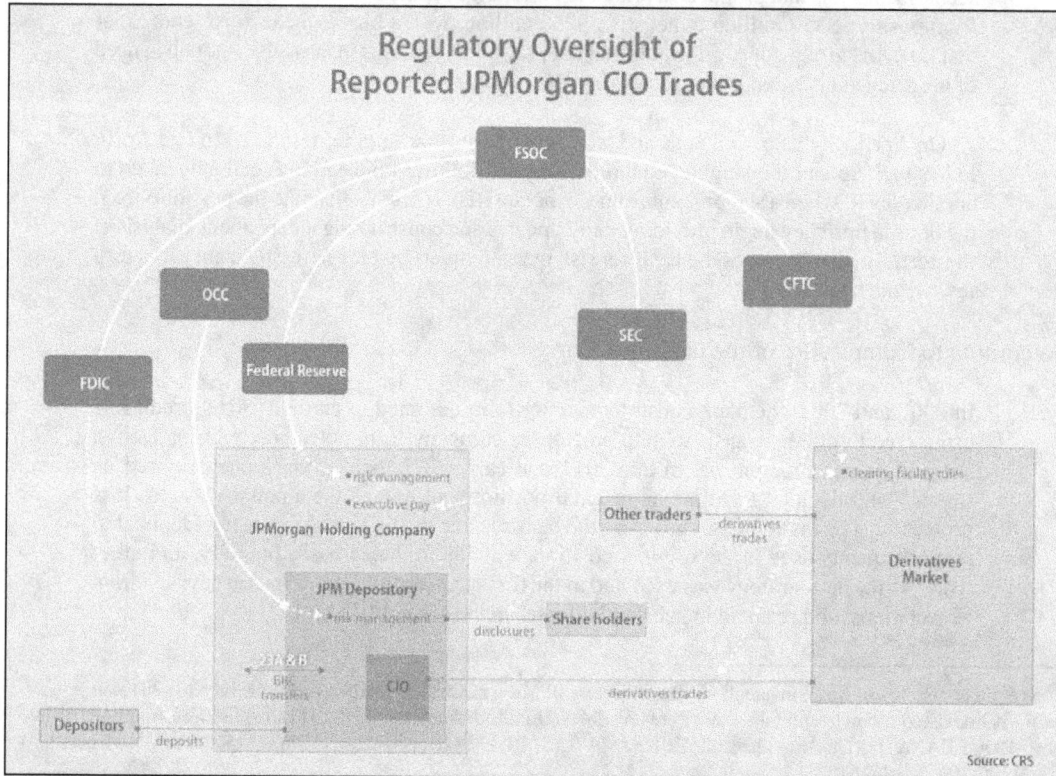

Source: CRS

The following is a more detailed explanation of the respective roles of the regulators that appear in **Figure 1**.

Office of the Comptroller of the Currency

The OCC is the primary prudential regulator for federally chartered insured depositories, including the relevant subsidiary of JP Morgan. Prudential regulators typically provide institution-based regulation, such as examination authority for safety and soundness. Insured depositories may be subject to the regulations of multiple prudential regulators; the primary prudential regulator depends on the firm's charter. Prudential regulators coordinate their examinations and standards through the Federal Financial Institutions Examination Council (FFIEC), of which the OCC is a part.

The OCC has a targeted large bank supervision program for complex firms such as JP Morgan.[46] The OCC's large bank program covers oversight of risk management, including expectations that the sophistication of a depository's risk management program match the complexity of the risks that the firm faces. The OCC testified to being in the process of raising these prudential standards, specifically to "increasing the awareness of risks facing banks and the banking system, reducing risk to manageable levels, and raising expectations for management, capital, reserves, liquidity, risk management, and corporate governance and oversight."[47]

At the June 6, 2012, hearing, the OCC provided information about its team that examines JP Morgan's depository subsidiary. The team includes 65 examiners onsite at JP Morgan, with additional support from other subject matter experts at the OCC.[48] The scope of these examiners' duties included reviewing all activities of the depository, "including commercial and retail credit, mortgage banking, trading and other capital markets activities, asset liability management, bank technology and other aspects of operational risk, audit and internal controls, and compliance with the Bank Secrecy Act, and anti-money laundering laws and the Community Reinvestment Act."[49]

As mentioned above, OCC officials have testified that they do not believe that the trading losses pose a significant threat to the solvency of JP Morgan or to the stability of the U.S. financial system. At the hearing, the OCC testified that the additional capital that JP Morgan has raised since the financial crisis provides a more than adequate buffer to prevent the firm from failing. Nor did the OCC find any evidence of contagion from the disclosure of the JP Morgan trades to concerns with other large U.S. banks.[50]

Federal Reserve

The Federal Reserve is the primary prudential regulator of JP Morgan's holding company. The bank holding company controls the depository subsidiary (and many other subsidiaries). Like the OCC, the Fed's examinations and regulatory standards are coordinated with other prudential regulators through the FFIEC. The Fed has had examination teams for large complex banking organizations (LCBOs) such as JP Morgan for more than a decade.[51]

The Dodd-Frank Act grants the Federal Reserve authority to regulate firms designated as systemically important financial institutions (SIFIs). SIFIs are sometimes referred to as too-big-to-fail firms, a designation that is controversial. Although implementation of this authority has not

---

[46] Testimony of Thomas J. Curry, Comptroller of the Currency before the Senate Committee on Banking, Housing, and Urban Affairs, June 6, 2012, available at http://www.occ.gov/news-issuances/congressional-testimony/2012/pub-test-2012-86-written.pdf - 2012-06-06.
[47] Ibid.
[48] Ibid.
[49] Ibid.
[50] Ibid.
[51] "Regulating LCBOs," Federal Reserve Governor Lawrence Meyer, January 2000, available at http://www.federalreserve.gov/boarddocs/speeches/2000/20000114.htm.

yet occurred, and JP Morgan has yet to be designated a SIFI, it appears likely that JP Morgan will be designated a SIFI when the appropriate rulemaking is final. The DFA instructs the Fed to establish heightened prudential standards for SIFIs, including more stringent standards for capital, leverage, and risk management.

The Federal Reserve is also the central bank of the United States. JP Morgan's depository has access to Fed lender-of-last-resort (LOLR) functions, such as the discount window. The Fed also has the ability to provide additional financial resources to troubled financial firms. The DFA mandates that such emergency credit facilities not be targeted to a single firm; rather, programs for extraordinary credit facilities must be made more widely available. This DFA provision prevents a JP Morgan rescue along the lines of the Maiden Lane arrangements that were created for Bear Stearns and American International Group (AIG) during 2008.

Federal Deposit Insurance Corporation

FDIC-insured depositories must comply with FDIC regulations. Although the FDIC is not the primary prudential regulator of JP Morgan's depository, the firm must still comply with all applicable FDIC rules. (The FDIC is the primary prudential regulatory for federally insured depositories with a state banking charter.) The FDIC coordinates prudential standards with the OCC and the Fed through the FFIEC. The FDIC has an interest in the standards supervised by the OCC and the Fed in part because the FDIC would have to compensate JP Morgan depositors in the event that JP Morgan failed with such large losses that there was not enough money to fully pay insured depositors.

The DFA grants the FDIC new authorities for SIFIs that fail. In the unlikely event that trading losses were to cause JP Morgan to fail, the FDIC could dissolve the entire firm, not just the depository subsidiary, if the failure threatened financial stability. Under the FDIC's resolution authority, JP Morgan shareholders and unsecured creditors would have to experience losses. However, the FDIC would not have to treat similarly situated creditors similarly, if doing so resulted in a threat to financial stability. JP Morgan counterparties to certain qualified financial contracts, including financial derivatives, would retain their ability to accelerate their contracts and net them out.[52]

General Concerns over the Bank Regulators and the JP Morgan Trades

The Comptroller of the Currency has testified that the CIO's "activities are conducted globally but managed and controlled out of JPMC's New York offices ... activities [that] are supervised by OCC staff assigned to the JPMC headquarters in New York." Questions have, however, been raised over the effectiveness of bank regulatory oversight and supervision surrounding the trades in question. For example, James Barth, the senior finance fellow at the Milken Institute and the Lowder Eminent Scholar in Finance at Auburn University, has commented:

> The huge loss at J.P. Morgan Chase, even if it grows to $4 billion or slightly higher, does not put a big dent in the overall financial soundness of the bank. Nor does it pose a systemic risk.

---

[52] CRS Report R40530, *Insolvency of Systemically Significant Financial Companies (SSFCs): Bankruptcy vs. Conservatorship/Receivership*, by David H. Carpenter.

> Our concern should be whether this is an isolated incident.... The solution is not tougher regulations based upon the J.P. Morgan Chase loss. Instead, it is the enforcement of existing regulations. Regulators already have the authority to prevent excessively risky activities. They simply must use that authority. If regulators won't use the powers they possess, what good does it do to give them even tougher powers?[53]

In this context, Senator Sherrod Brown has drawn attention to a letter he requested and then received from the OCC in which the agency reported that its examiners were not aware of the level of trading risks at the CIO until April 2012.[54] Fed Governor Daniel Tarullo has, however, suggested that it is unrealistic to expect bank regulators to track trades that are specialized in nature and that are relatively small in the overall context of a bank's activities:

> [W]e do already, within our supervisory process, look at market indicators, including aggregated market information, to try to identify trends that might be relevant to the particular institution. But that—our ability to do that obviously depends on the relative granularity or specificity of the information.... I think, in this case, for example, I believe there were products which, although they could be a big part of the market, JP Morgan could be a big part of a market, for the overall financial markets, were still relatively small. So unless there's reporting on more specific products like that, our normal look at market information wouldn't have—wouldn't have revealed this. So it has to come internally.[55]

Going forward, the OCC, JP Morgan's principal regulator, has said that it is

> Undertaking a two-pronged review of our supervisory activities and response. The first component is focused on evaluating the adequacy of current risk controls and risk governance at the bank, informed by their application to the positions at issue. The second component evaluates the lessons learned from this episode that could enhance risk control and risk management processes at this and other banks and improve OCC supervisory approaches.[56]

Securities and Exchange Commission

The SEC is the regulator for securities markets and corporate governance. The SEC also jointly regulates certain financial derivatives with the Commodity Futures Trading Commission (CFTC). As securities markets regulator, the SEC is not primarily concerned with the trading gains or losses of any single market participant; rather, the SEC's regulatory authority is primarily directed at ensuring appropriate disclosures by publicly traded firms, transparency and efficiency of trading platforms, properly aligned incentives for CEO compensation, and an absence of conflicts of interest by securities market professionals.

---

[53] James Barth, "Did Bank Regulators Miss J.P. Morgan's Risky Behaviors?," *U.S. News*, May 18, 2012, at http://www.usnews.com/debate-club/does-the-jp-morgan-loss-prove-the-need-for-tougher-bank-regulations/did-bank-regulators-miss-jp-morgans-risky-behaviors.

[54] See the comments of Senator Sherrod Brown in: "Senate Committee on Banking, Housing, and Urban Affairs Holds a Hearing on JP Morgan's Trading Loss." *Political Transcript Wire*, June 13, 2012.

[55] See the comments of Fed Governor Daniel Tarullo in "Senate Committee on Banking, Housing, and Urban Affairs Holds a Hearing on Bank Supervision and Systemic Risk," *Political Transcript Wire*, June 6, 2012, at http://search.proquest.com/docview/1018700192/13862F823951D3CD4A9/1?accountid=12084.

[56] Testimony of Thomas J. Curry, Comptroller of the Currency before the Senate Committee on Banking, Housing, and Urban Affairs, June 6, 2012, available at http://www.occ.gov/news-issuances/congressional-testimony/2012/pub-test-2012-86-written.pdf - 2012-06-06.

The SEC also has authority to enforce securities laws related to executive compensation. The DFA prohibits compensation that inappropriately rewards excessive short-term risk-taking.

SEC Chair Mary Schapiro has said that the JP Morgan trades in question did not occur in a broker-dealer supervised by the SEC and thus the agency has no direct oversight of the trades. Moreover, she has said that the agency does not oversee broad-based credit default swap indices, which are according to various reports at the center of the trades. She has indicated that the agency's inquiry into the trades will include an examination of the truthfulness and accuracy of JP Morgan's financial disclosure, particularly its earnings statements and its first quarter 2012 financial disclosures.[57]

Commodity Futures Trading Commission

The CFTC regulates certain financial derivatives activities, in some cases jointly with the SEC. This authority includes requiring certain derivatives to be standardized and traded through central clearinghouses and on exchanges.[58] It also includes regulating the safety of trading platforms, including elements such as position limits, capital, and margin. In some cases, CFTC authority might also extend to investigations of alleged market manipulation by some derivatives traders. Like the SEC, the CFTC is not primarily concerned with trading gains or losses of individual market participants. Rather, the CFTC generally requires that markets be transparent and free of conflicts of interest.

CFTC Chair Gary Gensler has said that the agency is responsible for regulating the "credit derivative products" and that the agency has launched a probe of the JP Morgan losses.[59] There have been some reports that the market in those securities may have suddenly become illiquid while JP Morgan was trading them. Among other things, the CFTC's probe may address whether the bank or its counterparties were responsible for or suffered from inappropriate or even possibly illegal market manipulation.[60]

Swap Dealer Registration. Title VII of the DFA gave the CFTC the power to require swap dealers and major swap participants (MSPs) to register and report to the CFTC and, similarly, the power to require security-based swap dealers (SBSDs) to register with the SEC. The goal of this appears to have been to bring swap dealers and their activities under more regulatory scrutiny. Testifying at the May 22, 2012, Senate Banking hearing, CFTC Chair Gensler noted that his agency had the authority to monitor credit derivatives markets for fraud and manipulation. However, he noted that the CFTC did not yet regulate JP Morgan as a swaps dealer because it had not yet finalized the DFA swap dealer registration rules. He then agreed with a committee member's description of the situation as a regulatory "no man's land."[61]

---

[57] For example, see "Senate Committee on Banking, Housing, and Urban Affairs Holds a Hearing on Derivatives Reform," *Political Transcript Wire*," May 22, 2012, at http://search.proquest.com/docview/1015167099/13801027F585D01F865/57?accountid=12084.

[58] CRS Report R40646, *Derivatives Regulation and Legislation Through the 111th Congress*, by Rena S. Miller.

[59] "Senate Committee on Banking, Housing, and Urban Affairs Holds a Hearing on Derivatives Reform," *Political Transcript Wire*," May 22, 2012.

[60] Ibid.

[61] Ibid. Going forward, JP Morgan's losses may help to expand the discussion on a number of derivative regulatory questions, including to what degree would such registration and reporting requirements for swap dealers to the regulatory make it more likely that the CFTC and SEC would be able to notice, or even prevent, such trading losses as (continued...)

International Coordination Issues. Title VII (§722(d)) of the DFA also states that reforms to swap markets shall apply to activities outside the United States if they have "a direct and significant connection with activities in, or effect on, commerce" of the United States. The CFTC reports that it is currently close to publishing a release on the cross-border application of swaps market reforms.[62] The release will provide interpretive guidance as to how swaps reforms apply to cross-border swap activities. It will include guidance as to when overseas swap market participants and swap dealers can comply with DFA reforms via reliance on comparable foreign regulatory regimes. Similarly, SEC Chair Schapiro stated that the SEC is working on a cross-border release expected to issue similar guidance, which will be released "soon."[63]

This issue is applicable to the JP Morgan situation because many of the trades were conducted in London, although the losses on the trades are expected to be absorbed by the U.S. holding company. Similarly, during the 2008 financial crisis, derivatives losses for AIG affected the U.S.-based holding company, resulting in a government-funded financial rescue—although most of AIG's derivatives losses were from transactions originating in London.[64] One policy issue that has been raised by CFTC Chair Gensler, at a hearing in May 2012, is how best to supervise overseas derivatives activities of U.S.-based firms with sufficient stringency, while enabling them to effectively compete with overseas firms that may have more operational flexibility.[65]

"Too Big to Fail" and the Financial Stability Oversight Council

JP Morgan's trading losses have helped to revive discussions over the doctrine of "too big to fail" financial institutions. This is the view that the federal government would not allow big, complex, highly interconnected institutions like JP Morgan to fail because the ensuing damage of such a failure to the nation's financial system would be devastating. Following the financial panic of 2008, the demise of the investment banking firm Lehman Brothers has figured prominently in discussions surrounding the doctrine's merits. More recently, referencing JP Morgan's trading losses, financial columnist Holman Jenkins contended that economic realities appear to dictate implicit national support for the doctrine:

> [I]f we're going to have a government-insured banking system that repeatedly encounters and perhaps causes financial turbulence, then having most of the risk concentrated in a handful of very large banks is a regulatory convenience. It makes it easier for Washington to stabilize the system by stabilizing just a few institutions.... The U.S. is committed to a system resting on a small number of giant, government-aligned institutions.... Central banks

---

(...continued)
JP Morgan's, by the largest financial institutions? Other than checking that the swap dealer has appropriate policies and procedures in place, how would this power to require registration ensure that regulators pay greater attention to large-sized, risky trades prior to rapid, large losses?

[62] Testimony of Chairman Gary Gensler Before the U.S. Senate Committee on Banking, Housing and Urban Affairs, May 22, 2012, available at http://banking.senate.gov/public/index.cfm?FuseAction=Files.View&FileStore_id= 10c178ef-a902-4842-9972-ca169eaceb7d.

[63] It was not clear from the May 22, 2012, testimony whether this is expected to be one joint SEC/CFTC release on cross-border activities or separate releases by each agency.

[64] See CRS Report R40438, *Federal Government Assistance for American International Group (AIG)*, by Baird Webel.

[65] Testimony of Chairman Gary Gensler Before the U.S. Senate Committee on Banking, Housing and Urban Affairs.

everywhere, trying to goose sluggish economies and prop up fragile banking systems, are creating giant pools of liquidity that must go somewhere. That some pooled up at J.P. Morgan, finding its way into a large, hedgeable portfolio of relatively safe corporate bonds, is hardly surprising.[66]

Others, however, say that the lessons that should be drawn from the bank's losses are at odds with the concept of "too big to fail." For example, Sheila Bair, senior advisor to the Pew Charitable Trusts and the former chair of the FDIC, observed,

> This is still a very serious issue. I think it does underscore that even with very good management these institutions are just too big to manage, and especially when dealing with very complex derivatives instruments trying to hedge risk in large securities trading books, even the best of managers can stumble. And so it does I think require, suggests smaller, simpler institutions, ones that have more focused management on particular business lines.[67]

A related part of the "too big to fail" discourse is a discussion on the implications of the losses for whether Congress should consider reinstating parts of the Glass-Steagall Act of 1933 (P.L. 73-66), also known as the Banking Act of 1933. The act separated commercial banking from investment banking, making them separate lines of commerce. Some have argued that JP Morgan's trading losses offer evidence on the desirability of separating commercial banking from investment banking through Glass-Steagall-like regulation. However, because JP Morgan's losses did not occur in the investment banking part of the firm, but rather occurred in a unit connected to the depository banking part, citing the bank's trading losses may not effectively advance the argument.[68]

To help monitor systemic risk in the financial system and coordinate several federal financial regulators, Title I of the DFA created the Financial Stability Oversight Council (FSOC). The council is composed of the heads of financial regulatory agencies and a state insurance regulatory representative.[69] The act also provides criteria for designating firms as systemically important financial institutions (SIFIs) and requires that SIFIs be subject to a number of heightened prudential standards compared with non-SIFI banks. The act also directs the Federal Reserve to monitor and regulate SIFIs, in addition to the functional regulators that supervise each SIFI subsidiary. As mentioned earlier, no financial institutions have yet been officially designated as SIFIs.

FSOC's proponents say that it was "established to promote a more comprehensive approach to monitoring and mitigating systemic risk."[70] Others, however, including Representative Jeb

---

[66] Holman Jenkins Jr. "The J.P. Morgan Distraction," *Wall Street Journal*, June 6, 2012, at http://online.wsj.com/article/SB10001424052702303830204577448472726957362.html.

[67] "CNN's Starting Point with Soledad O'Brien," *CNN*, May 14, 2012, at http://cnnpressroom.blogs.cnn.com/2012/05/14/shelia-bair-on-jp-morgan-fiasco-financial-institutions-are-too-big-to-manage/.

[68] For example, see Elizabeth Warren, "Warren Calls for a New Glass-Steagall Act to Protect Consumers from Wall Street Gambles," press release, June 5. 2012, at http://elizabethwarren.com/news.

[69] See CRS Report R42083, *Financial Stability Oversight Council: A Framework to Mitigate Systemic Risk*, by Edward V. Murphy.

[70] For example, see Speech by Vice Chair Janet L. Yellen at the Fourteenth Annual International Banking Conference, Federal Reserve Bank of Chicago, November 11, 2011, available at http://www.federalreserve.gov/newsevents/speech/yellen20111111a.htm.

Hensarling, vice chair of the House Committee on Financial Services, have characterized FSOC as a mechanism that bolsters what they consider to be the flawed doctrine of "too big to fail."[71]

If JP Morgan were designated a SIFI, a number of policy issues would apply. In particular, the DFA requires the Federal Reserve to monitor and enforce heightened standards for SIFIs for (1) risk-based capital, (2) leverage limits, (3) liquidity requirements, (4) resolution plan, (5) concentration limits, (6) contingent capital, (7) short-term debt limits, and (8) overall risk-management standards.

According to at least one regulatory official, FSOC discussed the JP Morgan trading losses, but did not believe that the losses were large enough to be a threat to JP Morgan's solvency or a threat to financial stability.[72] According to news reports, FSOC is examining the JP Morgan trading loss "so that mistakes in judgment at individual banks are less likely to threaten the broader financial system and economy."[73]

Systemic Implications of JP Morgan's Losses

Systemic risk refers to the possibility that the financial system as a whole might become unstable, rather than to the financial condition of individual market participants. It has been widely argued that stable financial systems do not transmit or magnify shocks to the broader economy. A firm, person, government, financial utility, or policy might create systemic risk if (1) its failure causes other failures in a domino effect; (2) news about its assets signals that others with similar assets may also be distressed, in what is frequently referred to as contagion; (3) it contributes to "fire sales" during asset price declines; or (4) its absence prevents other firms from using essential services, called critical functions.[74]

JP Morgan's trading losses are generally deemed to be too small to be a significant threat to current financial stability, a view shared by the officials from the OCC and the Treasury Department.[75]

Still, it could be argued that the JP Morgan trading losses illustrate a potential source of systemic risk. When large firms trade in markets with low volume, as reportedly was the case for the

---

[71] For example, Representative Hensarling has written, "Within Dodd-Frank's 2,300 pages are provisions allowing the government to designate certain financial firms 'systemically important financial institutions'—otherwise known as 'too big to fail' (TBTF).... Because private financial firms such as J.P. Morgan inevitably will blunder regardless of their size or sophistication, designating any firm TBTF is bad policy and worse economics. It causes erosion of market discipline and risks further bailouts paid in full by hardworking Americans. It also becomes a self-fulfilling prophecy, helping make firms bigger and riskier than they otherwise would be." Representative Jeb Hensarling, "When Risk is Outlawed; Rules that Ban Failure Will Also End Up Preventing Success," *The Washington Times*, May 18, 2012.

[72] See the comments of Neal Wolin, Deputy Secretary of the Treasury in "Senate Committee on Banking, Housing and Urban Affairs Holds a Hearing on Bank Supervision and Systemic Risk," *Newswire Political Transcript*, June 6, 2012, available at http://search.proquest.com/docview/1018700192/13801109260285B542E/3?accountid=12084.

[73] See Elizabeth Festa, "FSOC Examines Volcker Rule, JPMorgan Losses; Provides SIFI-Label," *National Underwriter Life & Health*, June 1, 2012.

[74] This section is drawn from CRS Report R42545, *What Is Systemic Risk? Does It Apply to Recent JP Morgan Losses?*, by Edward V. Murphy.

[75] Testimony of Thomas J. Curry, Comptroller of the Currency before the Senate Committee on Banking, Housing, and Urban Affairs, June 6, 2012, available at http://www.occ.gov/news-issuances/congressional-testimony/2012/pub-test-2012-86-written.pdf - 2012-06-06.

bank's loss-generating trades, they may have trouble liquidating their positions without affecting market prices. Under these conditions, their losses may be much greater than their risk-management models anticipated, if the models assumed normal conditions.[76]

The Potential Implications of JP Morgan's Losses for Other Large Banks

As Comptroller of the Currency Thomas Curry observed, "this asset-liability management function [the location of JP Morgan's CIO] is separate from JPMC's investment banking business, where most trading and market making takes place."[77] This quote helps emphasize the fact that, at JP Morgan and other LCBOs, most of the trading is done in their investment bank subsidiaries, not in CIO or CIO-like bank depositary-related units.

This is one reason why concerns have arisen over whether JP Morgan's losses signal the potential for problematic losses at other such banks as well. According to financial columnist Andrew Ross Sorkin,

> Well, the issue here in terms of why we should really care, the true context is that a Jamie Dimon, who's been exalted, as you said in your interview with him, as one of the great risk managers, to make a mistake, we've got a problem because it means that other banks could also make a mistake. And they could potentially make a mistake on a much grander scale. And who gets left holding the bag if that happens? The taxpayers.[78]

The same concerns arise for some who observe the environment in which large banks operate. The argument is that large banks such as JP Morgan are under pressure to make profits by investing in higher yielding but riskier securities in an environment in which there is muted demand for conventional commercial loans. Many of their potential corporate customers are hoarding their cash. An additional incentive to search for higher yield is said to come from the fact that safe investment alternatives like investment-grade government bonds currently have such low yields that it is hard for banks to profit from the yield spread between them and their deposits. In sum, it is argued that banks such as JP Morgan face heightened pressures to invest in riskier but potentially higher rewarding securities.[79]

On the other hand, at least two arguments have been advanced to refute the notion that JP Morgan's losses have any bearing on the likelihood of problematic losses at other large banks. One argument is that, time after time, banks' greatest exposure to losses has come from their loan making, not the kinds of trades that appear to have led to JP Morgan's losses.[80] The other

---

[76] Ibid.

[77] Ibid.

[78] Transcript for NBC's *Meet the Press*, May 13, 2012, at http://www.msnbc.msn.com/id/47403362/ns/meet_the_press-transcripts/t/may-reince-priebus-martin-omalley-gavin-newsom-al-cardenas-kathleen-parker-jonathan-capehart-chris-matthews-jamie-dimon/.

[79] For example, see Chris Mersey, "Shareholder Greed Explains JP Morgan Loss," *FT.com*, May 22, 2012, at http://www.ft.com/cms/s/0/96df65e2-9f7d-11e1-8b84-00144feabdc0.html#axzz1xv3sBeFl.

[80] Robert Samuelson, "Real Lesson of JPMorgan," *Orange County Register*, May 15, 2012, at http://www.ocregister.com/articles/crisis-354251-financial-banks.html.

argument is that, since the financial panic, the banking system has generally become significantly better capitalized.[81]

The Volcker Rule and JP Morgan's CIO Transactions[82]

Limits on Speculative Trades and Relationships by Banks

Section 619 of the Dodd-Frank Act is commonly referred to as the Volcker Rule, after Paul Volcker, former chairman of the Board of Governors of the Federal Reserve System, or the Merkley-Levin Amendment, after its sponsors, Senators Jeff Merkley and Carl Levin. It prohibits banking entities from engaging in proprietary trading[83] or affiliating with certain classes of firms that speculate in financial markets. This is an approach that Chairman Volcker advocated[84] and Senators Merkley and Levin pursued by introducing legislation in March 2010 that contributed to the development of the final language of Section 619.[85]

Under the conformance regulations, firms are not required to comply with the Volcker Rule until July 21, 2014. Since April 19, 2012, however, they are on notice that they are to engage in good faith efforts to achieve compliance by the 2014 date.[86]

One of the concerns of policymakers is whether the JP Morgan trading strategy that led to the recent losses would have been permissible were the Volcker Rule in force. At present, however, there is no final rule implementing the statute. In addition, it could be argued that there is insufficient specific information about the bank's transactions that resulted in the losses to meaningfully address that policy question even if the rules were in place. Also, there are some indications that the proposed rule that was issued by the agencies on November 7, 2011,[87] will

---

[81] See the comments of Eugene Ludwig, the CEO of Promontory Financial Group, and the former Comptroller of the Currency, in: Rob Blackwell, "A Giant Falls to Earth: JPM Losses Take Toll on Dimon," *American Banker*, May 14, 2012.

[82] Maureen Murphy, legislative Attorney in the America Law Division, significantly contributed to this section.

[83] Under the statute, "proprietary trading" is "engaging as principal for the trading account of the banking entity ... in any transaction to purchase or sell, or otherwise acquire or dispose of, any security, any derivative, any contract of sale of a commodity or contract, or any other security or financial instrument that the appropriate [agency] may, by rule ... determine." 12 U.S.C. §1851(h)(4).

[84] See CRS Report R40975, *Financial Regulatory Reform and the 111th Congress*, coordinated by Baird Webel.

[85] For a description of the provisions of S. 3098 and a summary of how the current statutory language evolved, see Senator Jeff Merkley and Senator Carl Levin, "The Dodd-Frank Act Restrictions on Proprietary Trading and Conflicts of Interest: New Tools to Address Evolving Threats," *Harvard Journal on Legislation*, summer 2011, pp. 534-539.

[86] "Conformance Period for Entities Engaged in Prohibited Proprietary Trading or Private Equity Fund or Hedge Fund Activities," 76 *Federal Register* 8365, February 14, 2011. Under these regulations a banking entity has two years, i.e., until July 21, 2014, to conform to the requirements of the law and may receive up to three one-year extensions upon application to the Board of Governors of the Federal Reserve System (Fed). On April 19, 2012, the Fed announced that currently "banking entities should engage in good-faith planning efforts, appropriate for their activities and investments, to enable them to conform their activities and investments to the requirements of section 619...." Board of Governors of the Federal Reserve System, "Statement of Policy Regarding the Conformance Period for Entities Engaged in Prohibited Proprietary Trading or Private Equity Fund or Hedge Fund Activities." Available at http://www.federalreserve.gov/newsevents/press/bcreg/bcreg20120419a1.pdf.

[87] 76 *Federal Register* 68846, available at http://www.fdic.gov/regulations/laws/federal/2011/11proposedNov7.pdf.

continue to evolve.[88] The language of the statute and the proposed regulation, however, provide insight into the multiplicity of details and complexity of documentation that would be required for a banking firm to justify a trade of the magnitude reported for the JP Morgan transactions as a risk-mitigating hedging activity.

With respect to proprietary trading, Section 619 states that "[u]nless otherwise provided in [Section 619], a banking entity shall not ... engage in proprietary trading."[89] It defines the term *banking entity* broadly to include bank and financial holding companies and their affiliates.[90] The trades resulting in billions of dollars in losses were executed by a JP Morgan unit that is part of a national bank, and, thus, a *banking entity* that will be subject to the Volcker Rule's ban on proprietary trading.

The proposed regulation generally tracks the statutory definition of proprietary trading[91] and defines *proprietary trading* as "engaging as principal for the trading account of the covered banking entity in any purchase or sale of one or more covered financial positions. Proprietary trading does not include acting solely as agent, broker, or custodian for an unaffiliated third party."[92]

Section 619's prohibition of proprietary trading attempts to prevent depository banks with access to the taxpayer-assisted safety net from speculating in financial markets. It can be difficult to distinguish a bank speculating for itself from a bank acting on behalf of customers or a bank hedging to improve safety and soundness. Section 619, therefore, provides for a number of exemptions, including but not limited to risk-mitigating hedging, trades in U.S. Treasury securities, market-making, and certain customer-driven services. Application and implementation of Section 619 will ultimately depend upon how financial regulators interpret proprietary trading and its exemptions.[93]

---

[88] In proposing the rule, the agencies sought feedback on 14 questions relating to the exemption for risk-mitigating hedging activities, among them "Is the proposed rule's approach to implementing the hedging exemption effective,?" and "Should additional restrictions, conditions, or requirements be placed on the use of the hedging exemption with respect to aggregated positions so as to limit potential abuse of the exemption, assist banking entities and the Agencies in determining compliance with the exemption, or otherwise improve the effectiveness of the rule?" 76 *Federal Register* 68846, 68876-68877, questions 102 and 109.

[89] 12 U.S.C. §1851(a)(1)(A).

[90] §619 applies to *banking entities*, a term that covers depositories, their holding companies, and all the affiliates in the financial or bank holding company. 12 U.S.C. §1851(h)(1). Under the proposed regulation, *covered banking entity* is defined in 76 *Federal Register* 68846, 68944, to include (1) any insured depository institution, except for trust companies meeting certain standards; (2) any company that controls an insured depository institution; (3) any foreign bank having a U.S. branch or agency, controlling a commercial lending company organized under state law, and parent company of such banks or companies; and (4) any affiliate or subsidiary of any of the above except for an affiliate or subsidiary that is a covered fund offered and held by the banking entity or an entity controlled by such a covered fund. See CRS Report R41298, *The "Volcker Rule": Proposals to Limit "Speculative" Proprietary Trading by Banks*, by David H. Carpenter and M. Maureen Murphy.

[91] Under the statute, *proprietary trading* is "engaging as principal for the trading account of the banking entity ... in any transaction to purchase or sell, or otherwise acquire or dispose of, any security, any derivative, any contract of sale of a commodity or contract, or any other security or financial instrument that the appropriate [agency] may, by rule ..., determine." 12 U.S.C. §1851(h)(4).

[92] 76 *Federal Register* 68846, at 68945, Subpart B.

[93] The statute permits the following activities, which might otherwise be considered proprietary trading: (1) trading in government obligations; (2) market making-related activities; (3) underwriting activities; (4) risk-mitigating hedging activities; (5) trading on behalf of customers; (6) trading by a regulated insurance company; and (7) trading outside the United States. These are permitted subject to the following conditions: (1) they are authorized under other law; (2) they (continued...)

One of the exemptions provided in Section 619 is for trades that are intended to reduce the risks of the bank. Specifically, Section 619 exempts "risk-mitigating hedging activities in connection with and related to individual or aggregated positions, contracts, or other holdings of a banking entity that are designed to reduce the specific risks to the banking entity in connection with and related to such positions, contracts, or other holdings."[94]

In general, the criteria attempt to ensure that the proposed trade is being used to offset risks to the bank's existing portfolio, not to take advantage of perceived new speculative opportunities. Among the qualifications are that the banking entity must already be exposed to the risk being hedged, that the hedge not earn appreciably more profits than the firm would lose on the hedged position, and that the hedge be reasonably correlated to the risk being hedged.[95]

Hedging to mitigate risks in a banking entity's portfolio is not only a regular activity but it is one that protects the banking entity's safety and soundness. In proposing the regulation, the agencies noted the difficulties in distinguishing risk-mitigating hedging from speculative proprietary trading retrospectively.[96]

As with any of the otherwise proprietary trading activities that Section 619 permits, risk-mitigating hedging activities are subjected to certain prudential backstops: (1) they may not be conducted unless they are authorized under other law; (2) they may be subjected to further limitations by the agencies; (3) they must not result in "a material conflict of interest" between the banking entity and its customers; (4) they must not result in a "material exposure by the banking entity ... to high risk assets or high-risk trading strategies"; and (5) they must not threaten the safety and soundness of the banking entity or U.S. financial stability.[97]

Deemphasizing the potential merits of the proposed rule, other observers such as Senator Richard Shelby, ranking Member of the Committee on Banking, Housing, and Urban Affairs, have suggested that it would be easier to ensure bank safety and soundness by simply ensuring that banks are subject to robust capital requirements.[98]

(...continued)
may be subject to further limitations by the agencies; (3) they must not result in "a material conflict of interest" between the banking entity and its customers; (4) they must not result in a "a material exposure by the banking entity ... to high-risk assets or high-risk trading strategies"; and (5) they must not threaten the safety and soundness of the banking entity or U.S. financial stability. 12 U.S.C. §1851(d)((2).

[94] 12 U.S.C. §1851(d)(1)(C).

[95] Under the proposed regulation, to qualify as a risk-mitigating hedging activity, a transaction must (1) comply with the banking entity's internal compliance program; (2) hedge one or more specific risks; (3) be "reasonably correlated, based upon facts and circumstances of the underlying and hedging positions and other risks and liquidity of those positions, to the risk or risks the purchase or sale is intended to hedge or otherwise mitigate"; (4) not give rise at its inception to significant exposures; and (5) be subject to continuing management review; (6) not be tied to compensation policies that reward "proprietary risk-taking." See the common rules section in 76 *Federal Register* 68846, 688948.

[96] 76 *Federal Register* 68846, 68874. "[R]isk-mitigating hedging activities present certain implementation challenges because of the potential that prohibited proprietary trading could be conducted in the context of, or mischaracterized as, a hedging transaction. This is because it may often be difficult to identify in retrospect whether a banking entity engaged in a particular transaction to manage or eliminate risks arising from related positions ... or to profit from price movements related to the hedge position itself...."

[97] 12 U.S.C. 1851(d)(2).

[98] "Senate Committee on Banking, Housing, and Urban Affairs Holds a Hearing on Bank Supervision and Systemic Risk." *Political Transcript Wire*, June 6, 2012, at http://search.proquest.com/docview/1018700192/
(continued...)

Some critics argue that the proposed rule is too permissive and will fail to prevent speculative trading.[99] They argue that a large and complex banking organization will likely be able to justify almost any speculative trade as being "reasonably correlated" to other positions held by the institution. Critics argue that the definition of hedge should be narrowed and that firms should not be able to justify trades by reference to the general condition of the banking entity.

Other critics argue that the proposed rule is too strict and will prevent legitimate hedging activities.[100] They point out that prudential hedging must address a variety of sources of risks, not just the risks of individual assets. For example, when a bank provides a loan commitment to an industrial manufacturer, the bank is exposed to counterparty risk (the risk that the manufacturer will default), interest rate risk (the risk that interest rates will move in a disadvantageous direction during the period of the loan commitment), and a number of other risks. These critics point out that the natural diversification of large portfolios makes measuring risk more complex. According to this perspective, firms should be able to use hedging strategies that address residual risks after a portfolio is netted, which might not be easy to document to satisfy the conditions in the proposed rule.

Criticism has been leveled by industry participants. Professor Hal Scott, for the Committee on Capital Markets Regulation,[101] sees the criteria as indicating "a belief on the part of the Agencies that hedging should be more precise a practice than it generally is, not producing excess profit or loss."[102] Morgan Stanley recommended that the agencies dispense with the "list of specific criteria because of the possibility of interpreting it as requiring the matching of principal positions with specific hedges," and adopt a more process-oriented framework.[103] PNC Financial Services Group Inc. (PNC) took issue with the implication in the proposal that proper hedges do not result in appreciable profit. It called upon the agencies to focus not on compensation, but on the purpose for which the hedge was transacted, and reminded the agencies that "the fact that the organization managed to effectively hedge its risks in a manner that also provides incidental profits to the organization promotes—rather than jeopardizes—the safety and soundness of the entity."[104]

(...continued)
13862F823951D3CD4A9/1?accountid=12084.

[99] For example, see Comment Letter on the Proposed Volcker Rule, submitted by Senators Jeff Merkley and Carl Levin to Mr. Robert Feldman, Executive Secretary, Federal Deposit Insurance Corporation, et al., February 13, 2012, available at http://www.fdic.gov/regulations/laws/federal/2011/11c228ad85.PDF.

[100] For example, see Comment on the Volcker Rule, by the Financial Services Roundtable, June 14, 2011, available at http://www.fdic.gov/regulations/laws/federal/2011/11c04ad85.PDF.

[101] The Committee on Capital Markets Regulation describes itself as an independent and nonpartisan research organization that seeks to improve the regulation of domestic capital markets. Its members come from the investor community, business, finance, law, accounting, and academia. The group's website is available at http://capmktsreg.org/.

[102] Hal S. Scott, Prohibitions and Restrictions on Proprietary Trading and Certain Interests in, and Relationships with, Hedge Funds and Private Equity Funds, February 13, 2012, available at http://www.sec.gov/comments/s7-41-11/s74111-281.pdf.

[103] Morgan Stanley, Comment Letter on the Notice of Proposed Rulemaking Implementing the Volcker Rule Proprietary Trading, February 13, 2012, available at http://www.regulations.gov/#!documentDetail;D=OCC-2011-0014-0304.

[104] PNC, "Prohibitions and Restrictions on Proprietary Trading and Certain Interests in, and Relationships with, Hedge Funds and Private Equity Funds," February 13, 2012, available at http://www.regulations.gov/#!documentDetail;D=OCC-2011-0014-0213.

JP Morgan Trading Losses in the Context of the Volcker Rule

JP Morgan criticized both the statute and the regulation as leaving "in doubt the protection of ... numerous legitimate asset-liability management hedging activities" and described some that it had used during the financial crisis that might not be exempt under the rule and that might be analogous to the type of hedging involved in the recent losses.[105] JP Morgan asserts that its losing trades, as described above, would qualify as a risk-mitigating hedge under the proposed rule. However, the Volcker Rule has yet to be implemented, so that it is not possible to test the bank's assertion.[106]

Going forward, there are several unanswered questions over the potential applicability of the not-yet-implemented Volcker Rule to scenarios such as the JP Morgan trades. For example, to the layman, hedging strategies are expected to lose money. Hedges are usually payments for protection from bad events—protection that the hedger hopes will not be needed. For example, if an airline signs a 10-year fuel contract at what it expects the long-run cost of fuel to be, and wishes to hedge against even higher fuel prices, then the airline might buy fuel derivatives. If fuel prices remain in the expected range, then the airline paid for protection, which it turns out it did not need, and the airline loses money on the hedge, but makes money overall. It would be very strange if people were surprised by announcements by airlines that they had lost money on fuel derivatives. The airline only expects to make money on the hedge if the price of fuel rises—which is bad for the airline overall; otherwise the airline expects to lose on the hedge.

It may be that the JP Morgan trade was indeed a hedge, but it has some elements that appear to violate the common understanding of a hedge. According to public disclosures, the JP Morgan trade was designed to profit the firm if economic conditions improved in the short run. Presumably, JP Morgan's general banking business is expected to perform better if economic conditions improve. Therefore, by itself, the described trade does not fit the common understanding of hedging as described above.

Modern risk management and modern banking regulation are more complex than the common understanding of hedging. Financial institutions are exposed to a variety of risks from a number of sources, some of which may occasionally move in opposite directions. For example, two of the risks that a bank faces when it extends a loan commitment are (1) the risk that the borrower will default (credit risk), and (2) the risk that interest rates will move in a disadvantageous direction during the period of the loan commitment (interest rate risk). In general, interest rate risk is usually correlated with general economic conditions and partially offsets default risk. Whereas a loan commitment to a manufacturer may be more likely to default during bad economic conditions, a loan commitment to a law firm specializing in bankruptcy cases may be less likely to default during bad economic conditions. Therefore, it is possible that there would not be a single best hedging strategy to address the performance of a portfolio of loan commitments in a

---

[105] JPMorgan Chase & Co., 'Re: Comment Letter on the Notice of Proposed Rulemaking Implementing Section 619 of the Dodd-Frank Wall Street Reform and Consumer Protection Act, also known as the Volcker Rule,' February 13, 2012, available at http://www.regulations.gov/#!documentDetail;D=OCC-2011-0014-0277.

[106] When the Volcker Rule is implemented, it will require examination of the firm's written policies, procedures, and testing, and the intent of the trade and the positions being hedged, that the firm be already exposed to the risk being hedged; that the hedge be reasonably correlated to that risk; and that the hedge not expose the firm to high-risk assets. In addition, the firm would have to "be prepared to identify the specific position or portfolio of positions ... being hedged and demonstrate that the hedging transaction is risk-reducing in the aggregate, as measured by appropriate risk management tools." 76 *Federal Register* 68846, 68875, common regulations §___.5(b)(2)(ii).

bad economic environment. In practice, banks are exposed to several other risks besides credit and interest rate risk, including but not limited to market risk, reputational risk, legal risk, and liquidity risks.

The JP Morgan CIO transactions might be a real hedge under this more nuanced appreciation for modern risk management. In addition to any correlations to JP Morgan's overall portfolio, a complex transaction might be used to manage the risk of another position that is slowly unwinding—which in the absence of full information might appear to "double down" on JP Morgan's overall portfolio. Or, a complex transaction might be used to manage residual counterparty risk or residual market risk even though the transaction does not address the firm's overall portfolio or correlate with a specific asset or liability. Without more details, competing characterizations cannot be ruled out.

In addition to issues raised at the firm level, the JP Morgan trades raise issues of congressional oversight. The complexity of modern risk management may make it difficult for Congress to monitor enforcement of the Volcker Rule by the financial regulators. Financial regulators do not generally comment on ongoing investigations or supervisory activities. As a result, it is difficult for a third party to confirm the facts of specific transactions or know how the regulators might apply the rules to specific firms or transactions.

Potential Risk Management Shortcomings Related to the CIO

Risk management involves the identification, analysis, assessment, control, avoidance, minimization, or elimination of unacceptable risks. Sound risk management is considered to be an integral part of bank safety and soundness. A key responsibility of bank regulators such as OCC is evaluating bank management's ability to identify and control risk. The importance of sound bank risk management has been underscored by Federal Reserve Chairman Ben Bernanke, who observed that, in addition to adequate bank management of its capital and liquidity, "the third key element of safe and sound banking ... is effective risk management. The [financial] crisis exposed the inadequacy of the risk-management systems of many financial institutions."[107]

The large reported trading losses at JP Morgan, a firm that enjoyed a reputation for quality risk management, have undermined its reputation and raised questions about the true nature of the bank's risk management. In response to a question about the possible meaning of the bank's losses, Treasury Secretary Tim Geithner responded, "I think this failure of risk management is just a very powerful case for financial reform."[108]

---

[107] Speech by Fed Chairman Ben S. Bernanke at the Federal Reserve Bank of Chicago Conference on Bank Structure and Competition, Chicago, May 7, 2009, available at http://www.federalreserve.gov/newsevents/speech/bernanke20090507a.htm.

[108] "Secretary of the Treasury Geithner Delivers Remarks at the Peter G. Peterson Foundation 2012 Fiscal Summit: America's Case for Action," May 15, 2012. By contrast, the Comptroller of the Currency merely indicated that, as part of the OCC's review of JP Morgan, "whether risk management controls, procedures, and reports were properly structured, reviewed, approved, and acted upon in the execution of this strategy is another focus of our ongoing examination...." Testimony of Thomas J. Curry, Comptroller of the Currency before the Senate Committee on Banking, Housing, and Urban Affairs, June 6, 2012, available at http://www.occ.gov/news-issuances/congressional-testimony/2012/pub-test-2012-86-written.pdf - 2012-06-06.

Based on media accounts and pending the conclusion of the various ongoing investigations into the CIO's trades, this report undertakes several tasks in this section. The report summarizes two developments that may have contributed to shortcomings in the risk management of JP Morgan's CIO and its trades: (1) Mr. Dimon's alleged emphasis on profit-making and attendant risk taking in the CIO; and (2) alleged potentially lax and ineffective oversight of trading at the CIO. It also examines two other developments that also have played a role in the diminution of the quality of the risk management: (1) alleged potential shortcomings in models used by the CIO to gauge the riskiness of trades; and (2) the composition of the risk management committee of the bank's board of directors, whose members may have lacked the experience necessary to effectively monitor the company's risk exposure.

CEO Dimon Allegedly Pushes for a Greater Emphasis on Profits and Risk Taking in the CIO

As noted earlier, various media reports allege that, after arriving at JP Morgan, Mr. Dimon played a key role in refashioning the CIO into a unit with a heightened emphasis on making profits by taking on greater trading risks.[109]

For example, one report stated that "Dimon pushed (Ina) Drew's unit ... to seek profit by speculating on higher-yielding assets such as credit derivatives .... The CEO suggested positions [and] [p]rofits surged over the next five years as assets quadrupled."[110]

Potentially Lax and Ineffective Oversight

Allegedly lax and ineffective oversight of the CIO's trades has been cited as a key potential contributor to the unit's perceived risk management shortcomings.

Mr. Dimon has testified that there were a number of risk management failings, including the following:[111]

- the "CIO's traders did not have the requisite understanding of the risks they took";

- "personnel in key control roles in CIO were in transition and risk control functions were generally ineffective in challenging the judgment of CIO's trading personnel";

- the "CIO, particularly the synthetic credit portfolio, should have gotten more scrutiny from both senior management and the firm-wide risk control function"; and

- each line of business at JP Morgan "has a risk committee. [The] risk committees and the head of risk in those businesses report to the head of risk of the company, and there are periodic conversations between the risk committees and the head of risk of

---

[109] For example, see Dawn Kopecki and Max Abelson, "Dimon Fortress Breached as Push From Hedges to Bets Blows Up," *Bloomberg*, May 1, 2012, and Jessica Silver-Greenberg and Ben Protess, "Gap Is Disclosed In U.S. Overseers In JPMorgan Loss," *The New York Times*, May 26, 2012.

[110] Linette Lopez, "This Explains How JP Morgan Changed Its Strategy And Became A Much Riskier Bank," *Business Insider*, May 14, 2012, available at http://articles.businessinsider.com/2012-05-14/wall_street/31695900_1_jamie-dimon-jp-morgan-s-ceo-dina-dublon.

[111] Testimony of Jamie Dimon, Chairman & CEO, JP Morgan Chase & Co., before the Senate Committee on Banking, Housing and Urban Affairs.

the company and [the bank's] ... senior operating group about the major exposures [they are] taking.... [T]hat chain of command didn't work in this case.... because ... [the firm] missed a bunch of these things.

Augmenting these observations, JP Morgan's July 2012 *CIO Task Force Update*, also found that

- during the first quarter of 2012, the CIO's management "did not set clear objectives, properly vet the trading strategy or sufficiently examine underlying positions and correlations";

- during the first quarter of 2012, CIO traders and managers of the problematic synthetic securities portfolio "did not adequately highlight issues or seek support from broader CIO or [JP Morgan] firm [level] management";

- the CIO's mandate and [its successful] historical performance may have "contributed to the less than rigorous scrutiny of the unit";

- during the first quarter of 2012, the CIO's review and analysis of the problematic synthetic securities portfolio "was too optimistic";

- the effectiveness of the CIO's risk management group was "challenged" by lack of a "robust risk committee structure"; "transitions in key roles"; and "lack of adequate resources";

- the CIO risk management group failed to "meet expectations" in various areas, including using inadequate risk limit levels, being insufficiently forceful in challenging the CIO's front office, and being insufficiently willing to communicate potential concerns over CIO risk-taking to top JP Morgan management; and

- the synthetic credit portfolio securities traded by the CIO problematically lacked "specific risk limits" and were subject to no limits on "size, asset type, or risk factor."

In addition, media accounts of comments by past and present JP Morgan employees provide other examples of potential risk management shortcomings at the bank's CIO, which could be associated with alleged lax and ineffective management. Although these news reports may provide some insights, the reader should keep in mind that observations based on personal recollections may be subject to errors of recollection, inaccuracy, and the potential for prejudiced observations.

- As early as 2007, reports indicated that some JP Morgan investment banking executives were raising concerns over the CIO's growing size and the complexity of many of its trades. In reports that some current JP Morgan officials dispute, some former JP Morgan officials have said that risk managers charged with overseeing the CIO's trades tended to be marginalized by Mr. Macris, the head of the CIO's London office. Generally supportive of Mr. Macris' management, Ina Drew, head of the CIO, was reported to have intervened sparingly in Mr. Macris' management of the office.[112]

---

[112] For example, see Jessica Silver-Greenberg and Nelson D. Schwartz, "Red Flags Said to Go Unheeded by Bosses at JPMorgan."

- In 2011, in what some say reflected aggressive risk taking, Mr. Macris reportedly unilaterally decided to abandon risk-control caps that had previously required traders to exit positions when their losses exceeded $20 million.[113]

- According to some media reports, in 2010, Joseph Bonocore, then-CIO's chief financial officer, reportedly grew concerned when he learned that traders at the London desk lost about $300 million on foreign exchange options during a few days, losses that had not been offset by offsetting gains. He supposedly took his concerns to Barry Zubrow, then-JP Morgan's chief risk officer, and Michael Cavanagh, then-bank's chief financial officer, both of whom reported to the CEO. Both men are reported to have authorized Mr. Bonocore to order a reduction to the trading position. The London desk reportedly complied with Mr. Bonocore's subsequent order to reduce the position.[114]

- JP Morgan's corporate treasurer reported to the bank's chief finance officer and managed the firm's balance sheet, capital, funding, and liquidity, and worked closely with heads of all its business lines. After 11 years as the CIO's CFO, Joseph Bonocore became the bank's treasurer in late 2010. His duties were reported to include weekly reviews of the CIO's trading positions. Reports say that before leaving the position of treasurer in October 2011, Mr. Bonocore expressed general concerns over the risks that the CIO's London office had been taking. After Mr. Bonocore left, the position of treasurer remained unfilled through March 2012, the period in which the CIO suffered the large reported trading losses.[115]

- Reports suggest that in 2011, several executives in the CIO's New York office developed some concerns that traders at the London desk were taking large trading positions in illiquid derivative indexes. Peter Weiland, then-CIO's chief risk officer, and some of his colleagues supposedly reportedly grew concerned that, if JP Morgan opted to sell the positions, it could incur significant losses. In late 2011, during a meeting of CIO management personnel, which was reported to include Ms. Drew, Mr. Macris, and Mr. Weiland, the group was reported to agree that the positions should be liquidated over the course of time. Subsequently, however, the London desk reportedly conducted new trades that appeared to contradict the directive.[116]

- During the summer of 2011, Mr. Weiland, then-CIO's chief risk officer, reportedly began an assessment of the CIO's risk limits, which included

---

[113] For example, see Monica Langley, "Inside J.P. Morgan's Blunder."

[114] For example, see Dan Fitzpatrick, "J.P. Morgan Knew of Trading Risks," *Wall Street Journal/Marketwatch*, June 11, 2012, at http://www.marketwatch.com/story/jp-morgan-knew-of-trading-risks-wsj-2012-06-11?reflink= MW_news_stmp.

[115] Reports based on comments from JP Morgan employees also said that during the vacancy, employees who had previously reported to Mr. Bonocore reported to the bank's CFO. A senior bank executive reportedly coordinated the day-to-day management of the treasurer's unit. Dan Fitzpatrick and Julie Steinberg "Key Void at Top for J.P. Morgan," May 17, 2012, at http://online.wsj.com/article/SB10001424052702303879604577410612215377958.html.

[116] For example, see Dan Fitzpatrick, "J.P. Morgan Knew of Trading Risks," *Wall Street Journal/Marketwatch*, June 11, 2012, at http://www.marketwatch.com/story/jp-morgan-knew-of-trading-risks-wsj-2012-06-11?reflink= MW_news_stmp.

discussions on whether restrictions needed to be tighter and more specifically delineated. According to the news reports, new limits were not implemented.[117]

- An article in the *Wall Street Journal* reported that, while he was the CIO's risk officer, Mr. Weiland told Ms. Drew that she needed to hire more personnel with credit risk skills and to allow those CIO credit risk officers who were engaged in other duties to focus on their jobs and not other tasks. Late in January 2012, Mr. Weiland was replaced as the unit's head of risk with Irvin Goldman, a former trader who the news accounts indicate had no experience as a risk manager and who was the brother-in-law of Mr. Zubrow, the bank's chief risk officer.[118]

- According to a number of reports, Ina Drew, the CIO's head, contracted Lyme disease in 2010 and took an extended leave in order to recover. During her absence, news reports said that the heads of the CIO's New York and London offices argued over the level of risk that the London office was taking, particularly the risks being taken by Bruno Iskil, a key trader in the office, who was nicknamed the "whale." Mr. Macris, head of the London office, was reported to ignore the cautionary concerns expressed by the head of the New York desk. When Ms. Drew, who worked out of New York, returned, it was reported that she was unable to reassert control over the London desk.[119]

Value at Risk Models and the CIO

As part of their risk management practices, banks regularly project the greatest potential losses that their portfolios might sustain during a given specific time frame, typically a day, or in a particular financial scenario, for a specific set of assumptions. Value at Risk (VaR) models are a standard means by which financial institutions like JP Morgan make such projections.[120]

Although regulators have designated VaR as the preferred method for measuring risk, they do not explicitly require financial institutions to use a standard or specific method.[121] Financial regulators, however, acknowledge that VaR calculations can take many different forms, and do not mandate the use of any particular VaR measurement. Still, every major financial institution measures and reports VaR.[122]

As the primary prudential regulator of federally chartered insured depositories, the OCC is also charged with overseeing their risk management. The OCC expects regulated banks to use appropriate VaR methodologies and to have appropriate internal controls in place to effectively manage risk. In some instances, VaR models are also used to help decide how much capital a bank will hold against trading its assets.

---

[117] Ibid.

[118] Ibid.

[119] For example, see Jessica Silver-Greenberg and Nelson Schwartz, "Discord at Key JPMorgan Unit Is Faulted in JPMorgan Chase's Trading Loss," *The New York Times*, May 19, 2012, at http://www.nytimes.com/2012/05/20/business/discord-at-jpmorgan-investment-office-blamed-in-huge-loss.html?_r=1&pagewanted=all.

[120] VaR models typically involve the use of a confidence interval of 95% or 99%. This means that, with an estimated 95% or 99% probability, a firm's losses will be less than the VaR value.

[121] "Overview of Risk Management in Trading Activities," *Federal Reserve Board*, 2000, at http://www.federalreserve.gov/boarddocs/supmanual/trading/2000p1.pdf.

[122] Ibid.

Mandatory SEC filings of publicly traded banks often include VaR-based calculations. Such disclosures inform investors seeking to assess a firm's financial health and the risks that it may confront.

During the May 2012 conference call, JP Morgan CEO Dimon announced that the bank was amending its disclosures in the first quarter 2012 press release concerning the CIO's VaR calculations. He said that the model that the CIO had used for several years to calculate the VaR was changed during the first quarter of 2012. The replacement model projected that the unit's extreme daily loss could be up to $67 million during the quarter. Mr. Dimon indicated that the replacement model was subsequently deemed to be "inadequate," and that the older model was better and had been restored. The older model showed the unit at risk of losing as much as $129 million a day, nearly twice as much as the subsequently abandoned replacement model.[123]

Historically, it appears that changes in the composition of portfolio assets, new information about the assets, or newer techniques for computing VaR may all prompt a company to change the way in which it measures VaR. By providing enhanced insight into corporate risks, such changes may benefit both investors and regulators. In addition to JP Morgan, other large banks such as Bank of America, Morgan Stanley, and Citigroup have also changed their VaR methodologies during the past several years.[124]

Still, concerns have arisen that the JP Morgan CIO's shift to the seemingly more optimistic VaR model during the first quarter of 2012 may have been a deliberate attempt to hide awareness of the level of risk that the CIO was taking on. Christopher Finger, a founder of the RiskMetrics Group, which helped pioneer VaR models, acknowledged that on occasion banks do modify their VaR models. He added, however, that these generally modest changes tend not to result in "dramatically different results." In this context, Mr. Finger noted that the older VaR model that the CIO reinstated reported "a huge, huge increase in risk" over what the earlier replacement model showed.[125]

On the general issue of their changing VaR models, Mr. Dimon observed that the company has "an independent model review group that looks at changes in models, and [that in the bank] … [m]odels are constantly being changed for new facts." Mr. Dimon also noted that "models are backward looking … [a]nd never are totally adequate in capturing changes in businesses, concentration, liquidity, or geopolitics or things like that. So we're constantly improving them."[126]

Later, however, among other things, the July 2012 *CIO Task Force Update* concluded that (1) the approval process for the problematic VaR model by JP Morgan's independent model review group was inadequate because of its reliance on parallel testing by the CIO and its use of unsuitable and overly optimistic assumptions; and (2) the implementation of the CIO's model's implementation by the CIO was undermined by operational challenges.

---

[123] See the comments of Jamie Dimon in Raw Transcript for JPMorgan Chase & Co., May 10, 2012.

[124] See Bank of America Corporation (2007, February 28) 10-K, retrieved May 31, 2012 from the SEC's Edgar database; Morgan Stanley (2007, February 13) 10-K retrieved May 31, 2012, from EDGAR database; and Citigroup Inc. (2005, February 28) 10-K, retrieved May 31, 2012, from EDGAR database; Citigroup Inc. (2004, March 1) 10-K, retrieved May 31, 2012, from EDGAR database.

[125] "JPMorgan To Be Haunted by Change in Risk Model," *Wall Street & Technology Online,* May 21, 2012.

[126] "Senate Committee on Banking, Housing, and Urban Affairs Holds a Hearing on JP Morgan's Trading Loss."

As part of its investigation of JP Morgan, the OCC may be interested in examining the corporate protocol used to authorize the changes to the CIO's VaR models. SEC Chair Mary Schapiro has emphasized that "when there are changes to the VaR model ... those changes have to be disclosed." As part of its probe of JP Morgan, the agency is likely to examine the accuracy and the timeliness of the bank's disclosures on changes to its VaR models for the CIO.[127]

JP Morgan's Risk Management Committee

Many financial firms have a risk management committee that is composed of members of the board. JP Morgan has such a risk committee. It is charged with approving its risk policies and overseeing its chief risk officer. According to company documents, the committee met seven times in 2011 and had the same three members between 2008 and the second quarter of 2012.[128]

As of May 2012, the three directors on JP Morgan's risk management committee were James Crown, president of Chicago-based Henry Crown and the lead board director of the General Dynamics Corporation; Ellen Futter, a former corporate lawyer and former chair of the New York Federal Reserve Bank from 1992 to 1993, who is currently president of the American Museum of Natural History;[129] and David Cote, CEO of Honeywell International. An article in *Bloomberg* reported that, unlike the risk committee of a number of other large domestic banks, no members of the committee reportedly worked at a bank or had been employed as financial risk managers. It also reported that the only committee member with experience on Wall Street, James Crown, the committee chair, reportedly has not worked in the industry in more than 20 years.[130]

Comparing the composition of the bank's risk management committee to its mandate, Anat Admati, a professor of finance at Stanford University who specializes in corporate governance, commented, "It seems hard to believe that this is good enough. It's a massive task to watch the risk of JP Morgan."[131]

According to a report from *CNBC*, in 2011, the CtW Investment Group, a union-based shareholder group, sent a letter to JP Morgan officials expressing concerns about the risk management committee. *CNBC* reported that the group complained that the panel had no one with expertise in "banking or financial regulation" and that it was "not up to the task of overseeing risk management at one of the world's largest and most complex financial institutions."[132]

---

[127] "Senate Committee on Banking, Housing, and Urban Affairs Holds a Hearing on Derivatives Reform."

[128] JP Morgan Chase Notice of 2012 Annual Meeting of Shareholders and Proxy Statement, April 4, 2012, at http://files.shareholder.com/downloads/ONE/1895794676x0x556146/e8b56256-365c-45aa-bbdb-3aa82f0d07ea/JPMC_2012_proxy_statement.pdf.

[129] In its 2012 proxy statement, JP Morgan indicated that her chairmanship at the New York Federal Reserve particularly qualified Ms. Futter for her job on the committee: "Such work ... [has] given her experience with regulated industries, in particular the financial services industry, and with risk management, executive compensation, and audit and financial reporting." Available at http://files.shareholder.com/downloads/ONE/1926409008x0x556146/e8b56256-365c-45aa-bbdb-3aa82f0d07ea/JPMC_2012_proxy_statement.pdf.

[130] Dawn Kopecki and Max Abelson, "JP Morgan Gave Risk Oversight to Museum Head With AIG Role," *Bloomberg*, May 25, 2012, at http://www.bloomberg.com/news/2012-05-25/jpmorgan-gave-risk-oversight-to-museum-head-who-sat-on-aig-board.html.

[131] Ibid.

[132] "JP Morgan was Warned Risk Management Not up to Task," *CNBC*, May 15, 2012, at http://www.cnbc.com/id/ (continued...)

At least one analyst, Barbara Matthews, a financial regulatory expert at BCM Regulatory Analytics in Washington, DC, asked whether the committee may have been out of JP Morgan's risk management "loop." She also observed, "If we find out that this is yet another example like AIG where information was not trickling up to the risk committee, that is one kind of risk management problem that frankly should have been addressed a long time ago."[133]

Mr. Dimon has defended the risk management committee, saying that it "did a great job," noting that it had successfully seen the company through the earlier financial panic. Mr. Dimon stated that the bank's board was replacing two committee members, and he also emphasized that it was unfair to blame the risk committee for the trade losses because it had depended on management to communicate key risk-based information to it, a responsibility that he said management failed to fulfill.[134]

The Dodd-Frank Act requires that each publicly traded bank holding company with $10 billion or more in assets establish a risk management committee entirely composed of independent directors. The committee is also required to have at least one member who is a risk management expert. As of July 2012, the Federal Reserve had not completed its rulemaking in this area.

Author Contact Information

Gary Shorter
Specialist in Financial Economics
gshorter@crs.loc.gov, 7-7772

Edward V. Murphy
Specialist in Financial Economics
tmurphy@crs.loc.gov, 7-6201

Rena S. Miller
Analyst in Financial Economics
rsmiller@crs.loc.gov, 7-0826

(...continued)
47436452/JPMorgan_was_warned_risk_management_not_up_to_task.
[133] Ibid.
[134] "Senate Committee on Banking, Housing, and Urban Affairs Holds a Hearing on JP Morgan's Trading Loss."